Tongues: God's Provision for Dynamic
Growth and Supernatural Living

12 Facts About the
Gift of Tongues

Patricia King

ISBN 978-1-936101-55-9

Published by XP Publishing
P. O. Box 1017
Maricopa, Arizona 85139
www.XPmedia.com

Printed in the United States of America

Contents

12 FACTS

ABOUT THE GIFT

OF TONGUES

DEDICATED TO ALL WHO HUNGER FOR MORE
OF THE HOLY SPIRIT AND HIS GIFTS

Tongues is a supernatural
God-given gift and ability
available to every believer.

The benefits are outrageous!

May the following twelve
facts about this glorious gift
grant you understanding
and build your faith enough
to receive, act, and enjoy
for the rest of your days.

FACT #1:

TONGUES IS A SPIRITUAL LANGUAGE

The gift of tongues is a spiritual language. It is the God-given ability to speak in a language that you do not understand. It is inspired of the Holy Spirit and could be an earthly language that is unknown to you, or a heavenly language.

> And they were all filled with the Holy Spirit and began to speak with other tongues, as the Spirit was giving them utterance.
> —Acts 2:4

> When this sound occurred, the crowd came together, and were bewildered because each one of them was hearing them speak in his own language.   —Acts 2:6

If I speak with the tongues of men and of angels...

—1 Corinthians 13:1

FACT #2:

TONGUES IS ONE OF THE NINE GIFTS OF THE HOLY SPIRIT

When Jesus was ready to depart, He promised His disciples that the Holy Spirit would come to empower them and be with them to lead, guide, direct, and empower others.

The Spirit came with gifts – nine of them: the gifts of tongues, interpretation of tongues, prophecy, word of knowledge, word of wisdom, discerning of spirits, faith, healing, and miracles.

The gift of tongues is one of these nine precious gifts the Spirit empowered His church with.

Behold, I am sending forth the promise of My Father upon you; but you are to stay in the city until you are clothed with power from on high. —Luke 24:49

But you will receive power when the Holy Spirit has come upon you; and you shall be My witnesses both in Jerusalem, and in all Judea and Samaria, and even to the remotest part of the earth. —Acts 1:8

But when He, the Spirit of truth, comes, He will guide you into all the truth. —John 16:13

For to one is given the word of wisdom through the Spirit, and to another the word of knowledge according to the same Spirit; to another faith by the same Spirit, and to another gifts of healing by the one Spirit, and to another the effecting of miracles, and to another prophecy, and to another the distinguishing of spirits, to another various kinds of tongues, and to another the interpretation of tongues.

—1 Corinthians 12:8-10

FACT #3:

A Gift Cannot Be Earned

Gifts are given to you. They are not earned. All that Jesus accomplished for us at the cross is a gift and therefore cannot be earned. Jesus gave us the fullness of all that He is and all that He has.

Tongues is a gift. You cannot earn it by striving or by performing enough good works to deserve it. It is a gift and therefore must be received.

It is possible for someone to send a gift to your home and yet when the postman comes to your door, you do not sign for it. Or perhaps you sign for it but it sits in the box and is never opened. Or maybe you went so far as to open the gift to see what was inside the box, but you never used it. When God gave the gift of tongues to His church, He wanted us to receive the gift, use the gift, and enjoy the gift.

Reach out to receive this precious gift. It has your name on it.

Every good thing given and every perfect gift is from above, coming down from the Father of lights, with whom there is no variation or shifting shadow.
—James 1:17

For by grace you have been saved through faith; and that not of yourselves, it is the gift of God; not as a result of works, so that no one may boast.
—Ephesians 2:8–9

While Peter was still speaking these words, the Holy Spirit fell upon all those who were listening to the message. All the circumcised who came with Peter were amazed, because the gift of the Holy Spirit had been poured out on the Gentiles also. For they were hearing them speaking with tongues and exalting God. —Acts 10:44–46

FACT #4:

THE GIFT OF TONGUES IS WITHIN EVERY BORN-AGAIN BELIEVER

All the gifts of the Spirit are inherent in the Holy Spirit. Therefore when you have the Holy Spirit, you have His gifts. His gifts are in Him and He is in you.

Jesus explained to Nicodemus that the way to enter the Kingdom of God was to be born again. He was not speaking of a natural birth but one of the Spirit. Jesus explained that the spirit man within us is the part that is born again by the Spirit of God.

When you ask Jesus Christ to enter your heart and become your Savior, His Spirit enters your human spirit and you become a brand new creation. This is called the new birth. You cannot be born into the Kingdom without the Holy Spirit.

When the Holy Spirit enters you, His life, abilities, and gifts come with Him. That means when you are born again, the gift of tongues is within you because it is within Him, but you need to unlock that gift and allow it to manifest through your life.

Jesus answered, "Truly, truly, I say to you, unless one is born of water and the Spirit he cannot enter into the kingdom of God. That which is born of flesh is flesh, and that which is born of the Spirit is spirit."

—John 3:5–6

I will ask the Father, and He will give you another Helper, that He may be with you forever; that is the Spirit of truth whom the world cannot receive, because it does not see Him or know Him, but you know Him because He abides with you *and will be in you*. —John 14:16–17

He who did not spare His own Son, but delivered Him over for us all, how will He not also with Him freely give us all things?

—Romans 8:32

FACT #5:

THE GIFT OF TONGUES IS OPERATED BY FAITH

Faith is the "connector" to every promise in the Kingdom. By faith you are saved. By faith you can receive the baptism of the Spirit (an infilling and saturation with the Holy Spirit that empowers you for service) and by faith you can operate in all nine gifts of the Spirit. The gifts are in you but they won't benefit the world around you if they stay within. These gifts must be released through you. How? By faith!

If you believe tongues is already within you, then your faith will enable them to become a great benefit to yourself and to others. Often, Christians who desire the gift of tongues are waiting for some special divine and sovereign intervention. But the Father gave His Holy Spirit to the church 2,000 years ago on the day of Pentecost. The Person of the Holy Spirit and His gifts are available for you to operate by faith. You can speak in tongues and enjoy all the benefits of this gift by faith … NOW!

These signs will accompany *those who have believed*: in My name they will cast out demons, *they will speak with new tongues.* —Mark 16:17

Blessed be the God and Father of our Lord Jesus Christ, who *has* blessed us with *every spiritual blessing* in the heavenly places in Christ. —Ephesians 1:3

Seeing that His divine power *has granted* to us everything pertaining to life and godliness ... For by these He *has granted* to us His precious and magnificent promises, so that by them you may become partakers of the divine nature, having escaped the corruption that is in the world by lust.   —2 Peter 1:3–4

Who by faith conquered kingdoms, performed acts of righteousness, *obtained promises...*
          —Hebrews 11:33

FACT #6:

WHEN YOU SPEAK IN TONGUES, YOU EDIFY YOURSELF

To edify means to build up, construct, or raise. When you pray in tongues, your spirit man (or inner man) is being empowered and built up in the Spirit. The more you pray in tongues the more you build up your spirit man.

As a new Christian filled with the Spirit, I prayed in tongues for hours at a time every day. Supernatural blessings followed. I had boldness to preach the gospel and experienced many divine appointments and "set-ups" by God. Words of knowledge and healings manifested, and the prophetic flowed freely. I cast out demons, and people were set free.

My mentor in the gifts of the Holy Spirit taught me to "charge up my spiritual battery" by praying in tongues. She emphasized that tongues empowers the operation of the other gifts of the Holy Spirit.

The more you pray in tongues, the more empowered you will be.

> One who speaks in a tongue edifies himself.
> —1 Corinthians 14:4

> But you, beloved, building yourselves up on your most holy faith, praying in the Holy Spirit... —Jude 20

FACT #7

When You Speak in Tongues, You Proclaim the Mysteries of the Kingdom

When you speak in tongues, your mind does not comprehend what you are speaking. It is an unknown language to your understanding. However, in your spirit you are speaking mysteries – the mysteries of the Kingdom.

There are many things that God wants to reveal to us, but we are not ready to understand them. By speaking in tongues we are decreeing these mysteries into the spirit realm so that the Spirit can bring revelation to us regarding these things. Therefore, in your spirit, you are becoming united with these glorious mysteries that will soon be revealed to your understanding. Tongues is a catalyst for receiving kingdom revelation.

> For one who speaks in a tongue does not speak to men but to God; for no one understands, but in his spirit he speaks mysteries. —1 Corinthians 14:2

> "I have many more things to say to you, but you cannot bear them now. But when He, the Spirit of truth, comes, He will guide you into all the truth; for He will not speak on His own initiative, but whatever He hears, He will speak; and He will disclose to you what is to come."
>
> —John 16:12–13

"Things which eye has not seen and ear has not heard, and which have not entered the heart of man, all that God has prepared for those who love Him." For to us God revealed them through the Spirit; for the Spirit searches all things even the depths of God.

—1 Corinthians 2:9–10

FACT #8:

WHEN YOU PRAY IN TONGUES, YOU PRAY A PERFECT PRAYER

How would you like to pray God's perfect will every time you pray? This is what you do when you pray in tongues. Your understanding is bypassed when you pray in tongues and therefore you cannot err. The prayer comes right up from your spirit man and is in perfect union with the will and purposes of God. In this way, you are actually praying the answers to your prayers. The devil cannot interfere by tempting you to pray amiss, so you hit the mark every time.

And He who searches the hearts knows what the mind of the Spirit is, because He intercedes for the saints according to the will of God. —Romans 8:27

For if I pray in a tongue, my spirit prays, but my mind is unfruitful. —1 Corinthians 14:14

This is the confidence which we have before Him, that, if we ask anything according to His will, He hears us. And if we know that He hears us in whatever we ask, we know that we have the requests which we have asked from Him. —1 John 5:14–15

FACT #9

WHEN YOU PRAY IN TONGUES, YOU OVERCOME HEAVINESS AND WEARINESS OF SOUL

Praying in tongues lifts and refreshes your spirit, and therefore heaviness and weariness leave. Before coming to Christ, I constantly suffered with bouts of deep depression and emotional weariness.

After I was filled with the Spirit, the Lord taught me to defeat those gripping forces through praying fervently in tongues. Whenever I felt heaviness of soul come on me, I would pray violently in tongues and it would leave. I was completely delivered from depression in 1980.

Since that time, I have found supernatural strength and refreshment through praying in tongues whenever I feel weary of soul, or even physical weary. Tongues grants you freedom and brings refreshing and rest to your soul. Heaviness and weariness leave.

Indeed, He will speak to this people through stammering lips and a foreign tongue, He who said to them, "Here is rest, give rest to the weary," And, "Here is repose."   —Isaiah 28:11–12

Come to Me, all who are weary and heavy-laden, and I will give you rest. Take My yoke upon you and learn from Me, for I am gentle and humble in heart, and you will find rest for your souls.
        —Matthew 11:28–29

FACT #10

WHEN YOU PRAY IN TONGUES, YOU OVERCOME WEAKNESSES

Have you struggled with weaknesses that you cannot seem to overcome? Well, tongues is a powerful key for you. When you pray in tongues, the Spirit will work victory within you by overcoming your weaknesses.

If you identify a specific weakness that you are wrestling with, begin speaking in tongues while focusing on your victory in that specific area. You will be amazed at the transformation.

My husband and I once instructed a man who was struggling with a pornographic addiction to pray violently in tongues for his break-through when he was tempted. He was set free through this act. It took a few months of diligent commit-ment to pray in tongues through each bombardment of temptation, but he did it! As a result, he experi-enced a fulfilling deliverance.

I have instructed many over the years to use this wonderful tool. As a result, people have overcome negativity, gossip, compulsive be-haviors, and gluttony (and as a result, have enjoyed major weight loss.) Identify a weakness and then pray focused tongues into your breakthrough.

In the same way the Spirit also helps our weakness; for we do not how to pray as we should, but the Spirit Himself intercedes for us with groanings too deep for words; and He who searches the hearts knows what the mind of the Spirit is, because He intercedes for the saints according to the will of God.

—Romans 8:26–27

FACT #11:

Tongues Is a Sign to the Unbeliever

When I first was filled with the Spirit and spoke in tongues, I shared my testimony with my friends. They were amazed and wanted to hear me speak in tongues. Tongues is a sign for the unbeliever. I have seen the gift of tongues cause many unbelievers to make inquiry about the gospel.

Sometimes, you can be speaking in the actual language of those around you when speaking in tongues, even though you do not understand what you are saying.

When we started ministering in Mexico years ago, we did not know the language, so we used inter-preters. One day, I was alone with a Mexican lady and there was no interpreter. She did not speak English and I did not speak Spanish, so we smiled at each other a lot.

The Spirit instructed me to speak in tongues to her. I felt a little unsettled and awkward but I obeyed. To my surprise, she understood. She kept saying, "Hallelujah, Hallelujah," while tears of joy streamed down her cheeks. I was not aware of what I was saying but continued.

A few minutes later our team returned and I called the interpreter over to give me insight on what I was saying in tongues. She said that I was declaring the greatness of God. I was extremely blessed.

I have seen this special gift of tongues touch many unbelievers since that time.

When we were in Africa, a missionary shared a story of how a "murderer-on-the-run" was convicted of his entire crime through hearing the missionary's daughter speak in tongues. She did not know that her tongues were declaring to this man the exact crime, the street where the murder took place, and all the details. He fell to the floor in deep, agonizing conviction. He then gave his heart to the Lord and turned himself in.

So then tongues are for a sign, not to those who believe but to unbelievers.
—1 Corinthians 14:22

FACT #12:

TONGUES + INTERPRETATION OF TONGUES = EDIFICATION FOR THE CHURCH

Most of the time the gift of tongues is to be used in a person's private prayer closet, as the gift has great personal benefit to the individual believer. However, the gift can also be used in public church gatherings.

In these situations, the gift of tongues must be accompanied by the gift of the interpretation of tongues so that everyone will be encouraged. In this sense, the gift of tongues with interpretation acts like a prophecy in its ability to edify the church.

Now I wish that you all spoke in tongues, but even more that you would prophesy; and greater is one who prophesies than one who speaks in tongues, unless he interprets, so that the church may receive edifying.

—1 Corinthians 14:5

FREQUENTLY ASKED QUESTIONS

Q. ISN'T TONGUES ONLY FOR SPECIAL INDI-
VIDUALS APPOINTED BY GOD? WHAT
ABOUT 1 CORINTHIANS 12:30, "ALL
DO NOT SPEAK WITH TONGUES, DO
THEY?"

A. All believers can speak with
tongues. First Corinthians
12:30 does not say all can't. It
says that all do not. Many believers do not speak in tongues,
but they can. They might not
know they have the ability, or
believe they have the ability, so
they do not step out in faith.

Q. DOES THE DEVIL UNDERSTAND ME WHEN I
SPEAK IN TONGUES?

A. When you speak in tongues, you could possibly be speaking in a heavenly language (language of angels) or an earthly language. Tongues is an "unknown" language to you. The devil was a high-ranking angel in heaven before he fell, so he knows all the angelic languages. He also is the tempter of mankind so he knows all the earthly languages.

Yes, the devil can understand, but he cannot intervene. You are praying a perfect prayer and making perfect kingdom decrees when you speak in tongues. He has no power to stop God's will that is proclaimed through tongues. He actually flees in terror.

Q. IS THERE SUCH A THING AS A COUNTER-
FEIT TONGUE? IS THERE A POSSIBILITY OF
SPEAKING IN A DEMONIC TONGUE WHEN
I WANT TO SPEAK IN GOD'S AUTHENTIC
GIFT OF TONGUES?

A. Yes, there is a counterfeit gift of
tongues in the same way that
there is counterfeit prophecy
and healing. The devil actually counterfeits everything
because he does not have the
power to create anything new.
You want to test the source of
all things, but you can be as-
sured that when you submit
yourself to God you will receive
from God and not from the devil. God is a good God and would
never give you anything evil.

The way individuals receive the counterfeit gift of tongues is to join the local witch coven or cult and submit themselves to a demon. When you submit yourself to God, He will give you what is holy. You do not need to fear.

Now suppose one of you fathers is asked by his son for a fish; he will not give him a snake instead of a fish, will he? Or if he is asked for an egg, he will not give him a scorpion, will he? If you then, being evil, know how to give good gifts to your children, how much more will your heavenly Father give the Holy Spirit to those who ask Him?   —Luke 11:11–13

Q. Will I be out of control when I speak in tongues? What will it feel like?

A. You will do the speaking but the Holy Spirit will give you the inspiration. You can stop and start at will in the same way that you can choose to pray in the language of your under-standing at will. You choose to speak in tongues or not to speak in tongues. It is your choice.

Some people feel a sensation or the presence of the Spirit but most people do not feel any-thing. Most believers do not feel any special sensations or unctions when they pray in the language of their understanding, either. Do not go by feelings. Speaking in tongues is an act of faith. You can pray in tongues whenever you desire and for as long as you desire.

Acts 2:4 clearly states that they spoke as the Spirit gave them utterance.

Q. I THOUGHT THAT TONGUES WAS NOT FOR TODAY BUT CEASED WHEN CHRIST'S ORIGINAL APOSTLES DIED.

A. Tongues have not ceased and will not until Jesus returns.

When the perfect comes, the partial will be done away.
—1 Corinthians 13:10

RECEIVE TONGUES
– IT IS EASY!

STEP 1:

RECEIVE JESUS AS YOUR PERSONAL SAVIOR, KING, AND LORD

In order to enter the Kingdom with all of its blessings, you must be born again. Jesus Christ is knocking at the door of your heart. Invite Him to come in and be your God. You cannot have more than one God. He must be your only God. Choose Him. When you receive Jesus as your Savior, King, and Lord, all the promises of the Kingdom are yours. If you desire to receive Christ and His gift of eternal life now, pray the following prayer:

Dear Lord Jesus, I come to You humbly, inviting You to enter my heart by faith and become my

Savior, King, and Lord. I turn away from all other gods and renounce them. I repent from my sins and ask You to forgive me and cleanse me of all unrighteousness. Thank You for coming into my life and making me brand new. AMEN.

If you prayed that prayer with sincere faith, Jesus came into your heart and gave you a brand new life. Your sins are forgiven and your name is written in the Book of Life in heaven. The Spirit of Jesus (His Holy Spirit) is now in your spirit man. He will never leave you or forsake you. All His gifts are in you.

Therefore if anyone is in Christ, he is a new creature; the old things passed away; behold, new things have come.

—2 Corinthians 5:17

STEP 2:

INVITE THE LORD TO FILL YOU WITH HIS SPIRIT.

It is one thing to have the Spirit of God take up residence within your spirit but another thing to have Him fill every part of your being. He will, if you invite Him. Ask Him to fill you – to immerse every part of you with His presence. This is called the *baptism with the Spirit*.

When you invite Him to fill your body, soul, and spirit, He will. This gives Him access to empower you for service. No longer will His presence only be in you but now will flow through you. Here is a prayer you can pray:

Lord, baptize me with Your Holy Spirit. I want every part of my being to be filled – body, soul and spirit. I surrender every part of my being to be filled, immersed, and overflowing with Your Holy Spirit. Fill me now. Amen.

But you will receive power when the Holy Spirit has come upon you; and you shall be My witnesses. —Acts 1:8

STEP 3:

BELIEVE

Believe that you now have Christ as your Savior, King, and Lord, that the Spirit of God has filled you, and that all His gifts are within you already – including tongues. Ask the Lord to help you release the gift of tongues.

Lord Jesus, I believe that I am Yours and that the gift of tongues is now within my spirit man. I choose to speak in tongues and activate this wonderful gift You have given me. Empower me now, as I desire to honor You with the release of this glorious gift. Thank You, Lord. AMEN.

He who believes in Me, as the Scripture said, "From his innermost being will flow rivers of living water."   —John 7:38

STEP 4:

ACT

Now remember that YOU have to do the speaking. That means it will be your voice and your mouth that forms the words. The Spirit gives the inspiration. This is an act of faith.

Begin to speak in tongues. Do not speak in the language of your understanding but speak sounds and syllables that you do not understand.

You might not feel any sense of empowerment at all, but remember, this is not about feelings or sensations. Just respond in faith in obedience to the Word. It is simply a matter of getting what is within, out. Let the sounds OUT.

> Even so faith, if it has no works, is dead, being by itself.
>
> —James 2:17

STEP 5:

BE CONFIDENT

If you have submitted yourself to the Lord in this process, you can have confidence that the words and sounds that come forth from your mouth are from Him. Do not let the enemy tell you, "Oh, that is not tongues, that is just gibberish." Command all doubt to leave.

Be confident and do not despise the days of small beginnings. When I first spoke in tongues I only had three syllables, but I was faithful to speak those three sounds every day. After a few weeks, a full language poured out of my mouth. God honored my faithfulness. He will honor yours.

Therefore I say to you, all things for which you pray and ask, *believe that you have received them,* and they will be granted you.   —Mark 11:24

STEP 6:

PRACTICE

Pray in tongues every day and more words will come. Be faithful and enjoy all the benefits of speaking in tongues.

> But solid food is for the mature, who because of practice have their senses trained to discern good and evil.   —Hebrews 5:14

If you received this wonderful gift, a brand new door has now opened for you. Enjoy a glorious future as you explore the fullness of His awesome Kingdom.

Cuma-shun-dai!

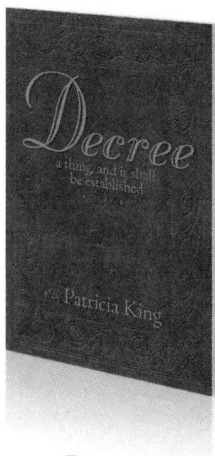

Decree
Decree a thing and it
shall be established! - Job 22:28

Activate the power of the Word in key areas of your life, including health, provision, love, glory, blessing, favor, victory, wisdom, family, business, spiritual strength and others.

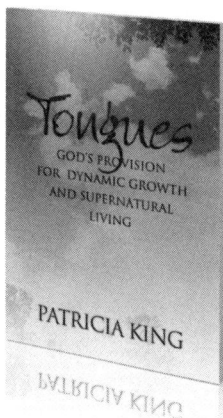

Tongues - God's Provision for Dynamic Growth and Supernatural Living.

Learn more about the key that unlocks the power of God within you, accelerates your growth and maturity as a believer, helps you enjoy deeper intimacy witht the Lord and much more.

Additional copies of this book and other book titles from Patricia King, XP Ministries and XP Publishing are available at the store at XPmedia.com

We have bulk wholesale prices for stores and ministries. Please contact: usaresource@xpmedia.com

For Canadian bulk orders please contact:resource@xpmedia.com

www.XPpublishing.com
A Ministry of Patricia King and Christian Services Association